By MeMoments Creative

This book belongs to:

Published in 2017 by
Createspace Publishing
USA

© MeMoments Creative

The Moral Rights of the author have been asserted.

All rights reserved. No part of this publication may be reproduced, stored, copied or shared by any means, electronic or physical, or used in any manner without the prior written consent of the publisher.

ISBN: 978-1544815718

Created by MeMoments Creative

Adult Coloring Books in The WTF?! Series

IVF WTF?!
Online Dating WTF?!

And more coming soon!

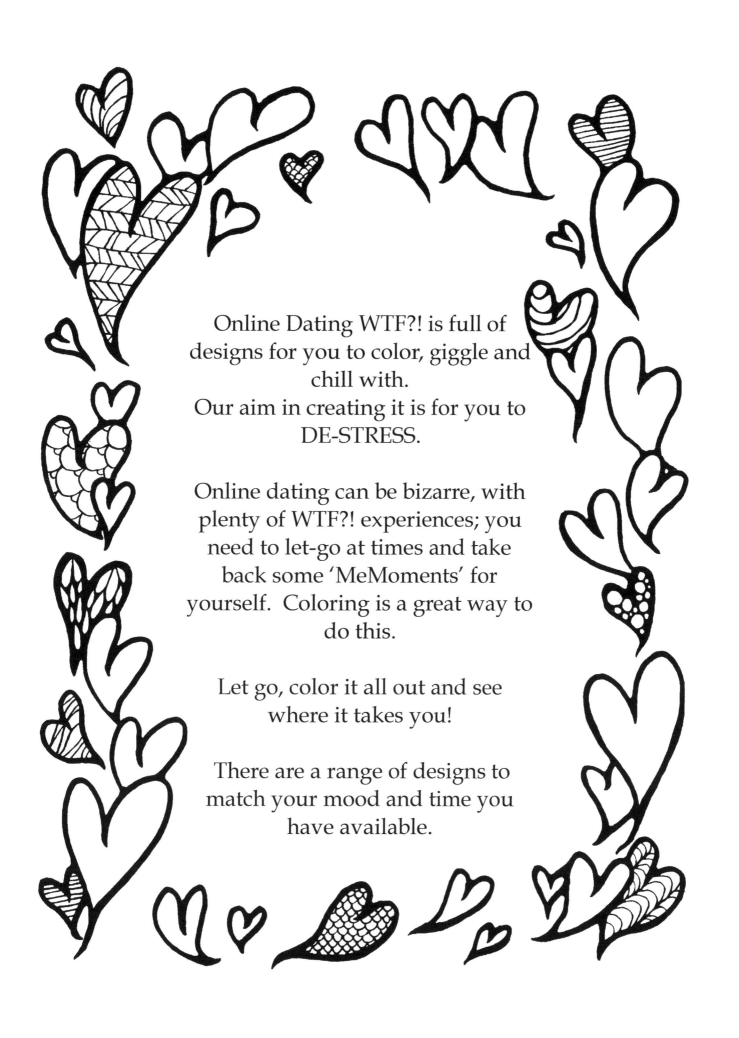

Online Dating WTF?! is full of designs for you to color, giggle and chill with.
Our aim in creating it is for you to DE-STRESS.

Online dating can be bizarre, with plenty of WTF?! experiences; you need to let-go at times and take back some 'MeMoments' for yourself. Coloring is a great way to do this.

Let go, color it all out and see where it takes you!

There are a range of designs to match your mood and time you have available.

Tester Page

Test your pens, pencils and coloring mojo on this page.

(The designs in the book are one per page to stop ink bleeding through. But to be safe, you can place a piece of paper or card behind the page you are coloring. This also works to prevent pressure marks from pencils.)

P.S. You can tear out and frame your coloring pages if you wish. Or you have our permission to photocopy the designs for your personal use if you want to try different colors, styles and tools for different moods you're in.

Please do share your work with **MeMoments Creative** on social media **(facebook.com/MeMomentsCreative)** and Instagram (**@MeMomentsCreative**). We would love to see what you come up with!

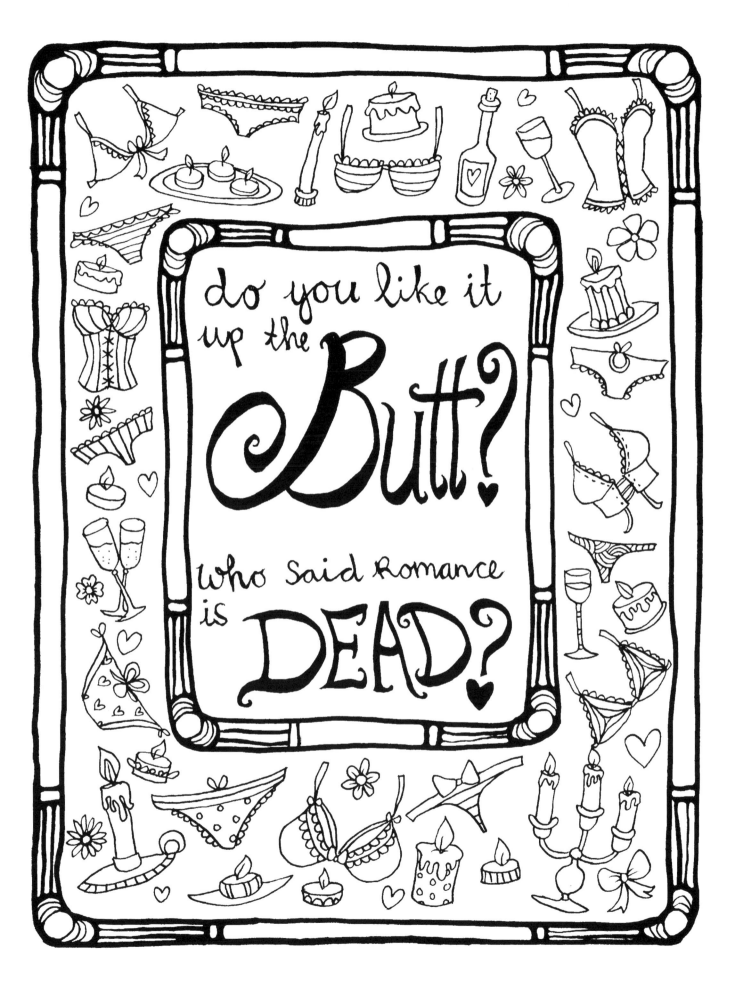

With love, from **MeMoments Creative.**
We hope you enjoyed coloring, had a giggle and de-stressed with the book.

If you did, we would really appreciate a rating and review on Amazon to help others find it too.

Please do share your designs with us over at: Facebook (**facebook.com/MeMomentsCreative**) and Instagram (**@MeMomentsCreative**)

And don't forget to try the other titles in the WTF?! series, or recommend them to anyone that might want (or need) to color, giggle and chill. (Don't we all!):

Titles
IVF WTF?!
ONLINE DATING WTF?!
More titles coming soon!

Made in the USA
San Bernardino, CA
04 March 2020